DIGGING UP THE PAST

POMPEII *and* HERCULANEUM

PETER HICKS

Thomson Learning • New York

DIGGING UP THE PAST

Biblical Sites • Bodies from the Past • Pompeii and Herculaneum • The Search for Dinosaurs • Troy and Knossos • The Valley of the Kings

Cover background: A view through the Forum at Pompeii with the volcano, Mount Vesuvius, in the distance

Cover inset: The plaster cast of one of the Pompeiian victims of the disaster in A.D. 79

Title page: Discoveries of fine public buildings and houses in Pompeii give us an insight into Roman architecture and lifestyles. This is a carving from the Odeon, or Small Theater (see page 20).

Contents page: The last moments of a guard dog were preserved for all time when this cast of its remains was made by Giuseppe Fiorelli (see pages 26–27).

First published in the United States in 1996 by
Thomson Learning
New York, NY

U.S. copyright © 1996 Thomson Learning

U.K. copyright © 1995 Wayland (Publishers) Ltd

Library of Congress Cataloging in Publication Data

Hicks, Peter, 1952–
   Pompeii and Herculaneum / Peter Hicks.
      p.   cm.—(Digging up the past)
   Includes bibliographical references and index.
   ISBN 1-56847-398-2
   1. Pompeii (Extinct city)—Discovery and exploration—Juvenile literature. 2. Herculaneum (Extinct city)—Discovery and exploration—Juvenile literature. 3. Time capsules—Italy—Juvenile literature. 4. Italy—Antiquities—Juvenile literature. I. Title. II. Series: Digging up the past (New York, N.Y.)
DG70.P7H53   1995
937'.7—dc20   95-24645

Printed in Italy

Picture acknowledgments

The publishers would like to thank the following for allowing their photographs to be reproduced in this book: Archiv für Kunst und Geschichte, Berlin 4, 8–9, 44 (bottom left); Camera Press Ltd. 15 (W. MacQuitty), 21, 39 (top) (G. Neri), 39 (bottom) (W. MacQuitty); C. M. Dixon Colour Photo Library *contents page*, 10, 27, 28 (both), 31, 33 (bottom), 45 (bottom right); E. T. Archive Ltd. 5 (top); Mary Evans Picture Library 13; Fine Arts Photographic Library 41; Robert Harding *cover background*, 37; Peter Hicks *cover inset, title page*, 5 (bottom), 6, 12, 14 (top), 16 (top), 17, 18, 19, 20, 23 (top), 24, 25 (bottom), 26 (inset), 30 (bottom), 33 (top), 34–35, 35, 36 (top), 38, 42, 43, 44 (bottom right), 45 (top, center, bottom left); Angelo Hornak 23 (bottom), 29, 40; Hulton Deutsch 8 (top), 14 (bottom); Roger-Viollet, Paris 16 (bottom) (© Collection-Viollet), 22, 25 (top) (© LL-Viollet), 30 (top) (© Harlingue-Viollet); Science Photo Library 7; Topham 20–21, 26 (botom). All artwork is by Peter Bull.

Contents

The First Discovery

One hot day in the summer of 1709, an Italian farmer named Joseph Nocerino—known as Enzecchetta—was digging out a well. Enzecchetta came from the village of Resina, in the shadow of the volcano, Mount Vesuvius, in southern Italy. While digging, he struck something very hard, and, looking down, he noticed some unusual stones. Enzecchetta knelt down and dug out beautiful pieces of white and yellow marble and alabaster stones from the soggy ground.

Enzecchetta was pleased with his finds because he could sell them for a good price. He sorted out the best pieces and headed for home. As soon as possible he contacted a *marmoraro*, a person who bought marble pieces and recarved them into statues for local churches or fountains. Satisfied with his sale, Enzecchetta probably thought no more about it.

From Decorations to Discovery

At that time Naples and southern Italy were ruled by Austria. An Austrian colonel, the Prince of Elbeuf, became engaged to a princess from Naples. He wanted to build an attractive villa for her in the countryside and fill it with beautiful objects and decorations.

◄ This bronze statue is typical of the type of treasure found in southern Italy during the eighteenth and nineteenth centuries.

▲ **This marble bust of Nero, Roman Emperor A.D. 54–68, is the type of object that was very popular during the eighteenth and nineteenth centuries.**

Later excavations at Herculaneum revealed the main street and the Basilica. The arch may have led to the Forum. ▼

Elbeuf contacted the *marmoraro* for a supply of marble and was told of Enzecchetta's finds. On visiting him at Resina the prince immediately bought all Enzecchetta's marble pieces, his well, and the nearby field. Elbeuf was convinced the land contained the ruins of an ancient building, so he called in an architect and feverishly started excavating. Very soon, tunnels were spreading out in all directions from the bottom of the well shaft. Workers found themselves among precious marbles, statues, vases, pillars, steps, and seats.

Elbeuf ordered the workers to sink the tunnels deeper and to take out every movable object. He believed he had discovered a single building, possibly a temple. Elbeuf was so obsessed with his search for treasure that he had no idea that he had actually discovered the Theater of the Roman town of Herculaneum—a town that had been violently and dramatically destroyed when Vesuvius erupted in August A.D. 79.

Disaster—Pompeii and Herculaneum Destroyed

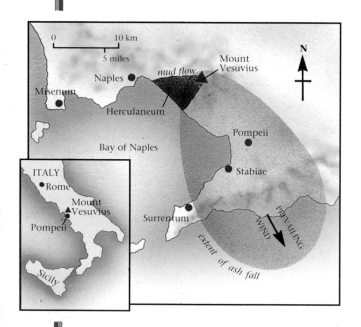

▲ **This map shows sites in the area around Vesuvius mentioned in this book. The shaded areas indicate the ash fall that covered Pompeii and the mud and lava flow that buried Herculaneum.**

Vesuvius, 4,190 feet above sea level, dominates the Bay of Naples. ▶

The Fateful Day Begins

The day the volcano erupted started like any other summer's day. As dawn broke over the Bay of Naples there were no clouds in the sky, the sea was a calm brilliant blue, and the green slopes of Vesuvius towered over the scene. True, there had been some earth tremors over the previous days and some wells and springs had dried up. Some people feared another serious earthquake similar to one that had taken place seventeen years earlier. But on this day, August 24, A.D. 79, the area seemed calm.

In two towns in the region, Herculaneum, a small coastal resort built on the lower slopes of Vesuvius, and Pompeii, a large country town farther to the southeast, people were beginning to go about their daily business. Very soon the towns were bustling with activity.

Shops and market stalls opened while women filled huge water jars from the many street fountains. The public baths, where the fires to heat the water had been lit earlier in the morning, were opening for business. The many wine bars, serving snacks of bread, lentils, figs, and nuts, as well as wine, opened their sliding doors to the streets. In Herculaneum a festival honoring Rome's first—and long-since dead—emperor, Augustus, was in full swing. In both towns, the many bakeries were open and people were busy buying fresh bread. At lunchtime in many houses families were gathering to eat. At a red-pillared house in Herculaneum the servants were serving hard-boiled eggs, bread, salad, and cakes. In Pompeii, at the Temple of Isis, the priests were sitting down to a meal of nuts, eggs, fish, and lentils.

Mount Vesuvius Erupts

Not much would be eaten, for suddenly a sickening, deafening crack split the air and the earth trembled violently. For a moment, people were stopped in their tracks. Those outside looked up toward the volcano and could not believe their eyes. Out of the summit, which had split wide open, poured smoke, fire, flaming lava, mud, and burning stones. Almost immediately, the day turned to darkness, and the sun was lost behind a thick veil of smoke. Fiery stones, raining down, started fires wherever they landed. Within seconds, the citizens in the two towns were plunged into confusion and panic.

▲ The violence of an eruption. This was the type of scene that brought terror to the people living around the Bay of Naples on August 24, A.D. 79. The lava headed down the slopes of Vesuvius toward the town of Herculaneum.

Eyewitness to the Disaster

We know all this happened because of an eyewitness. Pliny the Younger was about 17 years old at the time of the eruption and was staying at Misenum to the north of the Bay of Naples. Misenum was the base port of the Roman fleet, and the young man was staying with his uncle, the fleet's commander, Pliny the Elder. In two letters to the Roman historian Tacitus, Pliny the Younger gives a vivid account of the disaster.

▲ A portrait of Pliny the Elder (A.D. 23–79)

At first, Pliny the Elder, being an avid scientist, wanted to watch the eruption at close hand, but then he received a note from a friend's wife asking to be rescued. Realizing how serious the danger was he gave orders for a *quadrireme* (a four-decked galley ship) to be launched and sailed across the bay to help as many people as possible. Finding it difficult to land because of the now treacherous seas and mass of falling volcanic rock, Pliny ordered the ship to sail to Stabiae, a port on the southern point of the bay, to help another friend, Pomponianus. The situation at Stabiae was also becoming dangerous because of the rising levels of choking cinders and ash. Here Pliny the Elder became a victim of another danger from the erupting volcano. He was overcome by fumes and died while trying to escape to the shore.

This dramatic 1830 painting by Karl Brüllov, called *The Last Days of Pompeii*, captures the panic and fear the people of Pompeii must have felt during the disaster. ▼

Pliny the Younger had stayed at Misenum with his mother, but events there give us an insight into the blind panic that gripped the terrified population even though they were some distance from the eruption.

"The Darkness of a Sealed Room"

Early in the morning of the next day, August 25, the earth shook so violently that Pliny the Younger was afraid the walls of the house would collapse on top of them. He persuaded his mother to leave the town, but the streets were jammed full with hundreds of other people trying to do the same. The tremors continued. Although they were on level ground, carts "were tossed in every direction."

Suddenly a black cloud descended on the town and fearing his elderly mother would be crushed by the fleeing mob, Pliny and she made for the open fields. The thick black cloud surrounded them and day became night, "not [like] a moonless night, but the darkness of a sealed room."

In the terror of this nightmare, Pliny describes how many people prayed to the gods for help, "but a great number believed there were no gods and that this night would be the world's last."

It was disturbing to hear how all around people were calling for their lost families: "The shrill cries of women, the wailing of children, the shouting of men."

The above quotes are from translated letters by Pliny the Younger to the Roman historian, Tacitus.

Finally, the nightmare did end. A pale daylight returned, but with it came shock. Everything was covered by a thick layer of ash, similar to a heavy snowfall. What Pliny could not see from Misenum was that both Pompeii and Herculaneum were so completely covered by the outpourings of Vesuvius that the area looked level, as if the towns had never existed.

The Lost Towns

The Temple of Apollo was one of the fabulous buildings buried deep under ash in Pompeii. Apollo was the Roman god of light, music, and archery. The statue is a bronze copy of *Apollo the Archer*. The original was found inside the temple and is now in the National Archaeological Museum, in Naples, Italy. ▼

When the shocked survivors of the two towns returned to try to find their homes, an extraordinary sight greeted them. Herculaneum had totally disappeared under a massive layer of volcanic mud. At Pompeii, only the tops of the tallest buildings of the Forum—pillars, arches, and statues—poked out through a thick layer of ash and stone. The streets and buildings of this once wealthy town were nowhere to be seen.

Pompeii "Disappears"

On the day of the eruption the wind was blowing toward Pompeii, so the town received huge amounts of ash and volcanic stone, called lapilli. So much stone fell on to the roofs of the buildings that they collapsed under the weight. This must have killed or injured many people sheltering indoors. The fall of stone was followed by suffocating ash, which fell everywhere and lay over everything. The ash continued to fall for two days, so it is not surprising that Pompeii was sealed under 23 feet of this debris.

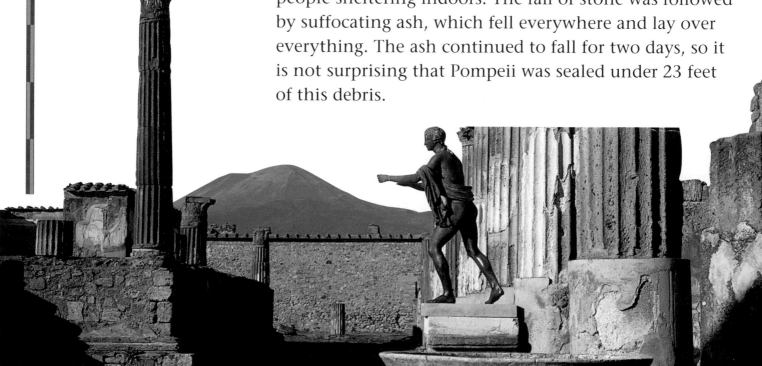

It has been estimated that 2,000 Pompeiians were killed in the disaster, out of a population of about 20,000. This figure is probably too low, for many people would have been killed in the chaos while trying to flee the city or drowned trying to escape across the rough seas.

Herculaneum's Fate

Herculaneum, being much closer to the volcano, suffered an even more terrible fate. When Vesuvius erupted, a river of ash, lapilli, and earth poured down in a boiling, bubbling volcanic mud flow. This slipped down the mountain and followed two stream beds that unfortunately passed either side of the town. For a moment, Herculaneum was an island in the midst of a torrent of flowing mud. Slowly the mud level rose and gradually covered every building and oozed into every room. It then cooled, forming an eighty-foot deep layer of solid rock. Later, returning survivors tried to cut through the rock into their lost homes, but gave up, exhausted.

Time Capsule

In this way, the towns of Pompeii and Herculaneum became sealed time capsules. Underneath the lapilli and the ash and rock the towns remained as they were on August 24, A.D. 79. Nature reclaimed the sites as weeds and plants, and eventually shrubs and trees, grew over the ash. The towns underground waited through the centuries to be discovered. The question was who would find them and would the sites be excavated properly?

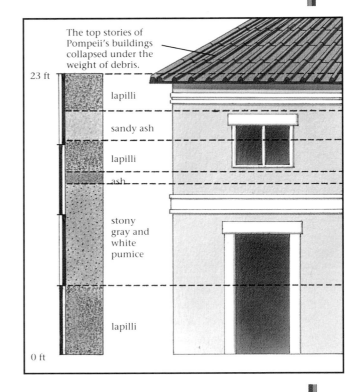

The top stories of Pompeii's buildings collapsed under the weight of debris.

23 ft

lapilli

sandy ash

lapilli

ash

stony gray and white pumice

lapilli

0 ft

▲ **This diagram shows the buildup of layers of volcanic debris that buried Pompeii.**

Discovery

▲ Once Vesuvius had become dormant (inactive), vegetation grew back and the area became good farmland. Generations of farmers must have plowed over fields that were covering Pompeii, and the village of Resina grew into a town above the solid rock covering Herculaneum.

As time passed, the two towns became a dim and distant memory. Local people told their children that once a terrible disaster had swallowed up the whole area, and this story was retold through the years. As the centuries passed, the story became a local legend, but no one knew with any certainty where the towns lay. The area hiding Pompeii was merely referred to as *la Città*—the City. The names of the two towns remained on old Roman maps, which were still being copied in the Middle Ages, but they were just names—the towns themselves were totally forgotten.

People Move Back

Vesuvius had not lain idle. It was fairly active and erupted on average once every hundred years. Because of the volcanic debris it deposited over the region, Pompeii and Herculaneum became buried even deeper. By 1400, the volcano quieted down and local people came to live on its slopes again. Villages and even small towns sprang up—the village of Resina was actually built on the rock over Herculaneum. Three hundred years later Enzecchetta would make his discovery of marble there.

Almost Found

A spectacular near miss occurred in 1593 when Count Muzzio Tuttavilla ordered the digging of an underground channel to carry water from the Sarno River to feed the fountains of his impressive villa at Torre Annunziata.

The most direct route for the channel was to cut across the site of Pompeii, in particular the Amphitheater, the Temple of Isis, and the Forum, which of course nobody knew were there. The workers hit upon marble fragments, coins of the Emperor Nero, and an important clue, a tablet with the inscription *decurio Pompeis* on it. This referred to a Pompeiian magistrate, but Count Tuttavilla believed the workers had stumbled on a villa once belonging to Pompey, a famous Roman general of the first century B.C. Six years were spent digging the channel but still the town of Pompeii remained a secret.

Charles III of Spain visiting the excavations at Pompeii in 1751. Charles' important visitors were given tours of the site and it was arranged for an impressive find to be "discovered" at the right moment. ▼

Herculaneum—Discovered at Last

We have learned how the Austrian Prince of Elbeuf mistook the Theater of Herculaneum for a temple. He gave up his plundering in 1716 when he thought there was nothing else worth finding. The Austrians were pushed out of Naples in 1734 by an army led by the Spanish Bourbon king, Charles III. As the "King of Naples and the Two Sicilies," Charles III showed great interest in the earlier discoveries of treasure by Elbeuf. In fact, he was prepared to invest a lot of his own money in future excavations.

Four years later, in 1738, when his new team was digging on the earlier workings over the Theater, Herculaneum was officially discovered. On December 11, an inscription was cut out of the rock explaining that "Lucius Annius Mammianus Rufus had, by his own money, built the Theatrum Heculansem" [the Theater of Herculaneum].

▲ A mosaic showing theatrical masks from the Theater of Herculaneum on display at the museum in Naples

Herculaneum was now officially back on the map. It seems extraordinary that this town, lying under so many feet of solid rock was discovered first, and that Pompeii, under 23 feet of lighter lapilli and ash, would have to wait another 25 years to be officially located. All this stemmed from Enzecchetta's digging out his well in his search for water.

The reign of Charles III was a very important factor in the discovery and uncovering of the towns. Throughout his reign (1734–59) the king showed a keen interest in the exciting finds and in excavating as much of the towns as possible.

The Theater of Herculaneum has been only partly excavated and is still underground. This 1779 diagram shows a cross-section view of the Theater and depicts the grand decorations, columns, and mosaics that had been found inside by that time. ▼

Treasure Hunters

Despite Charles III's keen interest, the problem at this time was that the engineers in charge of the digging did not act responsibly. They were more interested in finding valuable treasures and becoming famous than in learning more about the past for its own sake.

This solid gold Roman lamp was one of the treasures found at Pompeii. The search by treasure-hunters to find more items like this often led to the destruction of important, but less valuable, historical objects and structures. ▼

Damage Done

When in 1738 Charles III ordered further excavations to continue those started by Elbeuf, he made a great mistake. He appointed Chevalier Alcubierre, a Spanish engineer, to be in charge. Although he was a good engineer, Alcubierre had no idea how to excavate such a sensitive and important site as Herculaneum properly. Using pickaxes and even gunpowder, Alcubierre ordered his workers to open tunnels in all directions. Very soon the site became a maze of shafts, galleries, ladders, and sloping levels. Only the large, spectacular finds interested him—nothing else mattered.

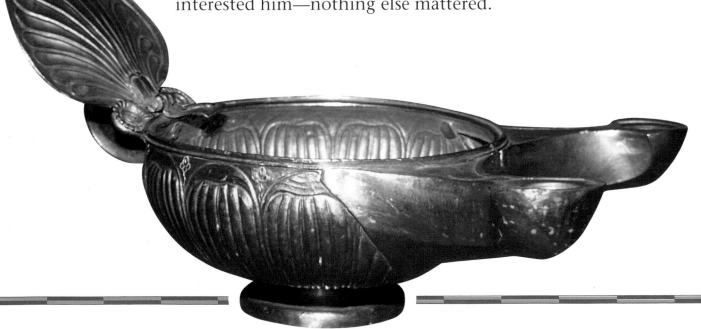

During all this plundering no detailed records were kept of the finds. In archaeology it is very important to record where objects were found, otherwise a "true" picture of the site cannot be built up.

At first no plans were made of the warren of tunnels, and, not surprisingly, even the workers got lost. In addition, Charles III had ordered that the discoveries be kept as secret as possible. Only a few people were allowed to sketch pictures of the finds and no one was allowed to write about them. The situation was chaotic. Very soon, even Charles realized that Alcubierre did not care about the historical importance of the site.

◄ Egyptian scenes were very fashionable in the Roman Empire. This beautiful floor mosaic shows birds and animals from the Nile River.

This engraving depicts excavation work during the mid-eighteenth century. ▶

Turning Attention to Pompeii

By 1748, the earlier rich finds at Herculaneum had all but dried up and the rock was proving very difficult to dig. Alcubierre tried to persuade the king to stop work at Herculaneum and to try their luck at *la Città,* where it was rumored local builders had hit upon some old walls, bronze statues, and ornaments. Charles agreed and Alcubierre switched to what he hoped would be an easier site to dig.

Alcubierre started work in March 1748 with twenty-four workers. They made some exciting finds: one a wonderful fresco of flowers, fruit, and vine leaves, perhaps from a dining room, and another of the first skeleton of a Pompeiian—a man with gold and silver coins near by. But Alcubierre was driven by greed and continued digging in all directions without care or thought.

In November work switched to an area to the east of the town. On the surface there was a huge oval dip in the ground that convinced Alcubierre there was a large building under the debris. Soon rows of seats were discovered and the team immediately recognized the layout of an amphitheater—although Alcubierre, obsessed with the idea he had found the old town of Stabiae, named it the Stabian Theater.

Because no silver or gold treasures were found at the site, the work at the amphitheater was abandoned in the hope of finding valuable treasure elsewhere.

The Amphitheater at Pompeii, which was wrongly identified by Alcubierre. The Amphitheater was an important center of entertainment—see page 42. In A.D. 59 a serious riot broke out among rival spectators that led to a ten-year ban on gladiator fights at Pompeii. ▼

Sense at Last

The situation was improved by the arrival on the scene of a Swiss architect, Karl Weber. Although working under Alcubierre, he began to develop much clearer ideas about the excavation of *la Città.* Alcubierre was jealous of Weber and was not above playing dirty tricks on him. When Weber had worked with Alcubierre before at Herculaneum, Alcubierre made sure the pit-props (wooden posts) of the tunnels were removed, causing the roofs to cave in!

Weber's ideas for excavation were a great improvement on the earlier chaos. He did not believe in widespread and disorganized digging. His exploration was carefully planned, concentrating on one area at a time. With this system, Weber was successful at *la Città,* finding the Gate of Herculaneum, which originally led to the road to the neighboring town. Finding this gateway suggested to Weber that there must be an important town in the area. Weber also found a large tavern, a mausoleum (family tomb) of a rich Pompeiian family, and the tomb of the priestess Mamia. At Herculaneum, Weber made the first drawings to record the galleries and buildings.

▲ The Arch of Caligula, in Pompeii. Each main street and gateway in and out of the town (see the plan on page 32) had a magnificent arch or gate like this.

Proof of Pompeii

On August 16, 1763, an important discovery was made. A statue of a man in a toga was dug up and on its base was a Latin inscription that read: "In the name of the Emperor and Caesar Vespasian Augustus, the Tribune T. Svedius Clemens has restored…to the public possession of the Pompeiians those places which belonged to them and had been taken into private possession." Here was definite proof that *la Città* was Pompeii and that a town was waiting to be uncovered. Unfortunately, in the same year Karl Weber died, but his place was taken by a Spanish engineer, Francesco La Vega.

▲ An impressive mausoleum in the cemetery by the Gate of Nuceria, Pompeii. If we look carefully in the niches we can see the busts of the people buried inside it.

More Damage

▲ The Odeon, or Small Theater. Notice the beautifully carved figure of a man "holding up" the wall at the end of the row of seats.

In 1765 the decision was made to shut down all work at Herculaneum and concentrate on Pompeii. This was decided not only because of the difficulty of cutting through the hard rock, but also because a gas was seeping through the galleries and caves and harming the health of the workers. With all the resources concentrated at Pompeii under La Vega some important buildings were located. In one small area, the Odeon—a small covered theater for concerts, the Great Theater, the Temple of Isis, and the Gladiator barracks were all found during the 1760s. La Vega felt that at last progress was being made.

The impressive Great Theater at Pompeii. Graffiti, telling us of the favorite actors of the day, show that plays and pantomimes were very popular entertainments in the town. ▶

Artifacts Lost Forever

While progress was made, it must be remembered that the methods of excavation on both sites had led to terrible damage and loss of precious artifacts. This was bound to happen when the excavators of the eighteenth and early nineteenth centuries, such as Elbeuf and Alcubierre, were simply hunting for treasure.

At most risk were the delicate frescoes. They were often hacked off the walls, only to fall apart while being moved to the king's museum. An art expert named Morriconi suggested covering the paintings with a thin varnish to keep them from fading and peeling. To the horror of the king, the varnish soaked up the paint, then dried, and flaked off! Morriconi was dismissed but the damage was done. After this, the king ordered that copies be made of each fresco. But many frescoes were not thought good enough for the king's collection and were either destroyed or reburied. The frescoes on display in the archaeological museum in Naples are probably only a fraction of the number actually found.

▲ One of the colorful frescoes from the superb Villa of the Mysteries in Pompeii. You can see some damage to the plaster, but the colors and detail of the fresco are almost as good as the day it was painted nearly 2,000 years ago. Many works like this were lost forever when Morriconi's ill-advised varnishing damaged them.

At Herculaneum, under Alcubierre, pieces of a racing chariot and some bronze horses were discovered. A sculptor named Joseph Canart was brought in to restore them, but having inspected them he decided they were beyond repair. Instead of restoring them he melted down the body of the charioteer and cast it into medals, figurines of saints, and ornaments.

This disregard for the importance of the finds led to the destruction of many of the artifacts. Much of the archaeological record of the two towns was lost forever.

Papyrus Books—Turned to Dust

A wonderful villa was discovered at Herculaneum in 1752. In one of the rooms were found burned cupboards containing blocks of charred papyri. One worker picked a bundle up and they immediately turned to dust. They were in fact papyrus rolls—Roman books—and a huge library containing almost 1,800 rolls had been found; but reading them was going to be difficult. A priest from the Vatican library named Antonio Piaggi designed a machine for unrolling the scripts. He was hastily brought to Naples, but in four years of painstaking work he only pieced together three rolls while dozens more were destroyed.

Learning the Lesson

This is one of the tragedies of Pompeii and Herculaneum. In many ways they were discovered too soon, before modern methods of excavation and conservation had been developed. As a result the losses have been great. Even today, archaeologists leave sections of large sites unexcavated so that future generations, perhaps with better technology than we have at the moment, can do a better job.

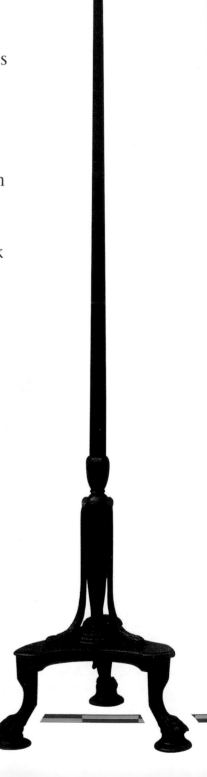

Some wonderful bronze objects, such as this stand from Pompeii, still survive but many were broken up or melted down during the time Alcubierre was in charge of the site. ▶

Giuseppe Fiorelli and His Followers

With the death of Francesco La Vega in 1815, the excavations slowed down considerably. Antonio Bonnuci, an Italian architect, was put in charge, but by 1818 he had only thirteen workers under him. Despite this the 1820s proved to be a fruitful period of discovery.

The Forum with its many temples and monuments was finally uncovered, and the last part of the Gladiator barracks was cleared in 1823. A year later, the Temple of Fortuna Augusta and the Forum Baths were located. Bonnuci himself found the House of the Faun.

▲ The *caldarium*, or hot room, of the Forum Baths, Pompeii. The basin was used for washing hands before bathing. It is dated A.D. 3–4.

◄ Many rich Roman houses had openings in the roof to catch rainwater in a basin, or *impluvium.* This *impluvium* is completed with a copy of the original faun (a part-goat, part-human creature) that gave the house its name, The House of the Faun, Pompeii.

On October 24, 1831 a sensational discovery was made at the site. This was the huge, finely detailed mosaic of *Alexander at the Battle of Issus*. It consists of about one and a half million colored stone cubes each measuring between one-eighth and one-fourth inches across. After months of careful work, the mosaic was taken from the floor and is today on display in the museum in Naples. It depicts the famous Greek general, Alexander the Great (356–323 B.C.), in the midst of battle.

Fiorelli Appointed

Momentous events were to affect Pompeii and Herculaneum in the second half of the nineteenth century. In 1860, the Bourbon dynasty in Naples and Sicily was overthrown and the Italian king, Victor Emmanuel II, took the throne. The new king, aware of the importance of Pompeii and Herculaneum to Italy, put a young coin expert, Giuseppe Fiorelli, in charge of the renewed excavations. Fiorelli took control on December 20, 1860 and by January 7, 1861 there were 512 workers on the site. Fiorelli was to revolutionize the whole field of archaeology and introduce scientific principles to excavation.

Cleaning Up the Mess

At Pompeii, Fiorelli immediately addressed the problem of waste, or "spoil," as archaeologists call it. The site was a mass of pits, garbage dumps, and buildings left open to the weather. It was totally confusing to any visitors. The first task Fiorelli gave the workers was to clear away all the earth, ash, and lapilli, in order to join up all the half-excavated sites. (A small railroad was built to help them.) Then roofs were built over the sites for protection from the sun, wind, and rain. Only when this was done did Fiorelli begin new excavations. He divided Pompeii into regions made up of groups of buildings—called *insulae* (meaning islands). This system is still in use today.

He also introduced a *Journal of the Excavations of Pompeii* to replace the old diary of royal visits and lists of finds. In the journal were written detailed descriptions of finds, their position when found, the depth or layer in the ground, as well as any possible conclusions.

▲ This photograph shows work being carried out in Pompeii in 1863.

The mills and oven of a bakery in Pompeii ▼

Let the Work Begin

Once this system was in place, Fiorelli ordered new excavations. As the west of the town was almost totally uncovered, the excavators methodically moved eastward. During this time they discovered a House of Pleasure, or brothel, a wonderfully preserved bakery—Fiorelli himself rescued 81 blackened rolls from an airtight oven—and the house of a banker named Lucius Caecilius Jucundus.

The First Plaster-Cast Bodies

Fiorelli gave strict instructions to his workers that if anything interesting or unusual was found, work should stop and he should be told immediately. One day in 1864, his workers discovered a cellar, containing a skeleton, in a side street between the Baths and the Forum. Fiorelli arrived and examined the skull, noting that the rest of the body was hidden in the hardened crust of volcanic ash. He realized that if plaster of Paris was poured into the cavity (hole) made by the body, a mold of the dead body could be taken.

This was done, and when the plaster dried and the other debris was removed, four plaster casts of the cellar's inhabitants remained. The group consisted of two females, possibly mother and daughter—the mother protecting her daughter with an outstretched arm. Beside them were three pairs of gold earrings, more than a hundred silver coins, and two iron keys. Another woman, wearing a simple iron ring, and a huge man, wearing sandals, were also present.

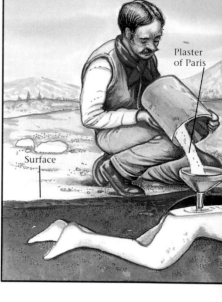

▲ **How a plaster-cast body was made**

It is still a shock for many visitors to see the suffering on the victims' faces, preserved after nearly 2,000 years. ▼

◀ **The victims, either overcome by fumes or suffocated by ash, died where they fell.**

Outline of a body left in the ash

Making Plaster Casts

How did this process work? When people were overcome, usually by the strong sulfur fumes, some were covered with damp ash, which became solid while the body was still intact. The outlines of the body were therefore preserved as a hard mold, and when the body decayed only the skeleton remained inside. It was into this space that Fiorelli poured the plaster of Paris.

The great advantage of this method of excavation was that as well as the reconstruction of the body's shape, the impressions of clothing, shoes, and facial expressions appeared. The last moments of the unfortunate victims on that fateful day were preserved for all time.

Some of these remarkable reconstructions have been left exactly where they fell, while others have been removed to the Pompeii museum. The workers who found the side street containing all these bodies gave it a nickname—*vicolo degli scheletri*—"skeleton alley."

In 1869, Fiorelli began excavations at Herculaneum. Once again progress was slow because of the rock, and in 1875 work stopped. In the same year, Fiorelli was made general director of all Italian excavations and museums and moved to Rome. The two men who succeeded him at Pompeii and Herculaneum, first Michel Ruggiero and then Giulio de Petra, were his students and well-taught in Fiorelli's methods.

This cast is of a guard dog found outside one of the houses in Pompeii. ▼

The Banker and the Wax Tablets

One of the first discoveries that Ruggiero had to deal with was from the House of Lucius Caecilius Jucundus, the Pompeiian banker. An iron chest was found containing 132 wooden Roman writing tablets. They were covered by a thin layer of beeswax, and words were scratched on the wax with a metal pen— a stylus. Although some of the wax was missing, the impression of the stylus was scratched into the wood, so 127 of the tablets could be read. They were mostly business receipts kept by Jucundus and contained many signatures of well-to-do Pompeiians.

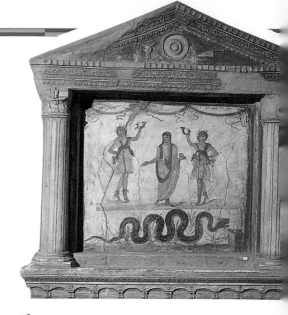

▲ All houses were protected by local gods. This shrine, on a wall of the Vettii house, carries the familiar snake that represents the household gods.

The Vettii Villa

In 1893, Giulio de Petra began his direction of the site and had the good fortune to oversee the excavation of Pompeii's most famous building—the House of the Vettii brothers. This has now been almost totally restored. With its impressive peristyle, which is a group of columns and frescoes surrounding the courtyard and garden, it is easy to imagine the comfortable life of these brothers and their families who made their fortune selling wine.

The garden of the House of the Vettii brothers, in Pompeii. The roof supported by columns was a popular style of Roman architecture. ▶

The Twentieth Century

The scientific approach to excavation was continued into the new century. By now a lot more time and care was being taken over the digging, and the spoil was sifted before it was removed to make sure no small finds had been missed. Obviously this method was a great improvement although it was very costly.

During the time Antonio Sogliano was director of the site there was more interest in the conservation of Pompeii. Any houses that were damaged were restored in as accurate a way as possible. Taking a lead from Giuseppe Fiorelli, Sogliano wanted to restore a house or shop in such a way that when one entered it, it would seem as if the owners were still living there. So frescoes and mosaics remained where they were found—but were protected by guards against theft. Shops like the wine bars—*thermopolia*—looked as though they were ready to serve a thirsty and hungry Pompeiian a drink and a snack.

▲ The huge fresco in the House of Lucius Secondus, Pompeii. It shows lions hunting various prey—a bull is being chased in the foreground. African landscapes were very popular subjects in the Roman Empire.

▲ This picture shows Vittorio Spinazzola showing visitors the newly excavated Street of Abundance in 1910.

The garden of the House of Loreius Tiburnitus, Pompeii. It is superbly landscaped. ▼

The Street of Abundance

Vittorio Spinazzola, the director from 1910–24, was determined to abandon the excavations in the north of Pompeii in favor of work to the south. His great plan was to connect the center of the City—the area around the Forum—with the Amphitheater and the Gate of Sarno to the east. This would uncover the business heart of the city through the excavation of the appropriately named Street of Abundance.

The beginnings of the excavations went extremely well— the first industrial workshop in a private house was found. This was the workshop of a fuller (who cleaned and dyed cloth), complete with a tank for washing cloth. An impressive *thermopolium* (wine bar) was uncovered, with bronze containers for the drinks set into the bar, a lantern hanging from the ceiling, and some money left on the counter. One house found on this street belonged to Marcus Loreius Tiburnitus. He had built a huge garden at the back containing water channels and an open-air *triclinium* (dining room) with frescoes on the walls.

Of course, if he hoped to excavate along 2,000 feet of street front, Spinazzola had to limit himself to the façades of buildings on both sides of the street. He could not excavate inside the dwellings or learn the exact layout of shops.

Instead he had to try to decipher the curious graffiti and election slogans that covered many of the walls. Some of these writings were very clear and gave insight into what life was like in a Roman town.

Excavating the street first gave rise to a serious problem: the façades of the buildings threatened to collapse. They had to be reinforced against the pressure from the mass of damp earth behind them. After 1,300 feet were cleared, the excavations had to be stopped, and they remain in this state today.

▲ A street in Pompeii. Many houses facing the street did not have windows because of the constant noise from the carts driving over the cobbles. Notice the raised sidewalks, which kept pedestrians out of the muddy winter roads.

Effect of World War I (1914–18)

When World War I began in 1914, Italy was not involved, so excavations continued. However, after Italy joined in the war in 1915, work slowed down. In the political turmoil that hit Italy after the war ended in 1918, it is not surprising that the excavations suffered.

In 1925, Benito Mussolini came to power and set up a fascist dictatorship that destroyed the democratic political system in Italy. One of the many aspects of fascism is nationalism, that is, a strong belief in one's country. Mussolini promised his people "Glories like those of ancient Rome," so he injected new energy into excavations. Amedeo Maiuri, who had worked under Sogliano and Spinazzola, had been appointed director in 1924, and he was to remain in the post until 1961.

Stratigraphic Excavation

Stratigraphic excavation is very common in modern archaeology. It involves stripping a site down by layers. It follows that the deeper the layer the older it is. An artifact found in a much deeper layer would therefore be older than an artifact found in a layer near the surface.

Using this stratigraphic method, Maiuri was able to learn that the Temple of Jupiter, at the north end of the Forum, originally had a totally different design and structure. Underneath the fine buildings to the east of the Forum there had once been a row of very ordinary shops.

A plan of the street layout of Pompeii with sites discussed in this book ▼

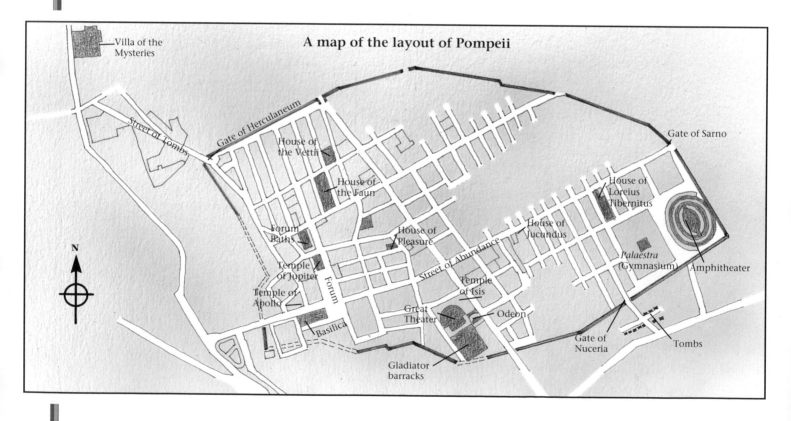

A map of the layout of Pompeii

Herculaneum

Because of the very special problems of Herculaneum—the depth of the rock and the worries of the people of Resina regarding damage to their houses—work was halted in 1875. However, in 1927, the government gave permission for excavation to start again.

Vesuvius's outpourings had formed new land that had pushed the sea back. The idea behind the 1927 excavation was to work between the original waterfront of A.D. 79, to the south, right up to the houses of Resina, to the north. It was believed that the town probably stood over the area of the Forum and Basilica. Amedeo Maiuri was able to speed up the work by the introduction of electric boring-machines and mechanical shovels. Electric saws (to cut blocks of stone), bulldozers, a narrow-gauge railroad and numerous trucks were also used. Modern mining techniques were replacing the old fashioned pick-axe, shovel, and wheelbarrow. It was the aim of Amedeo Maiuri to reclaim and then restore Herculaneum as closely as possible to its original state. He joked that if an inhabitant of the town could come forward in time he should be able to find his house in as good a condition as when he left it.

▲ The northern end of the *Palaestra*, or Gymnasium, in Herculaneum

The House of Stags. This is probably the most luxurious house in the south of Herculaneum. ▼

How Big Were the Towns?

During Maiuri's leadership and from 1961 to the present day, three-fifths of Pompeii's 163 acres have been uncovered, but only four *insulae* have been completely excavated at Herculaneum. This raises another question. How big was the town? One calculation based on the size of the theater, discovered in the eighteenth century, puts the population at roughly 5,000. This would suggest the area of the town is about a third of that of Pompeii, around 55 acres. However, these figures are really only guesses.

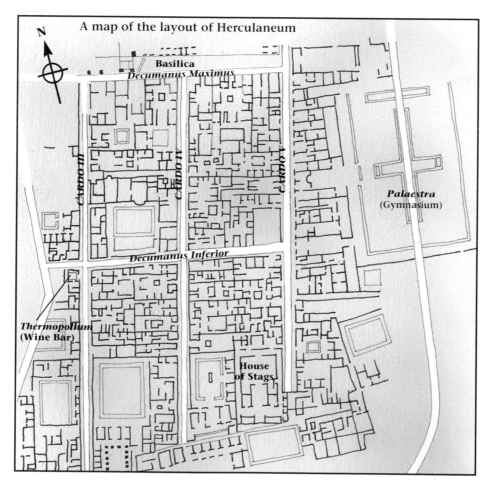

A map of the layout of Herculaneum

N

Basilica
Decumanus Maximus

CARDO III

CARDO IV

CARDO V

Palaestra
(Gymnasium)

Decumanus Inferior

Thermopolium
(Wine Bar)

House
of Stags

▲ *Cardo* was the name given to any street that crossed a Roman town from north to south. At the north end of *Cardo IV* in Herculaneum, the depth of the solid rock can clearly be seen.

A charred entrance to a wine-seller's shop ▶

Top Stories

Interestingly, the volcanic mud that slowly engulfed the town helped preserve many of the upper stories. Today in Herculaneum it is common to see many overhanging first stories—a rarer sight in Pompeii. This was because in Pompeii the weight of the lapilli destroyed the roofs, and in turn dragged down the upper stories with them.

Stopping the Decay

There is also a lot more original wood in Herculaneum. Volcanic mud at a temperature of about 1,800 °F came into contact with the wood in the houses. This set the wood on fire and charred it. As the mud rose it put out the flames and sealed the wood away from the air. As a result, the wood did not rot. Even now that doors, stairs, and even pieces of furniture are out in the open, the layer of burned wood keeps them from rotting.

Too Late to Escape!

Because of the small number of skeletons found at Herculaneum, it was always believed that the slow movement of the volcanic mud had allowed most of the population to escape with their lives (and perhaps some of their possessions).

In 1980 a discovery was made that showed that not everyone was lucky enough to get out alive. Some workers digging a drainage ditch located a group of skeletons on the original beach.

When the archaeologists began excavating, they discovered 139 skeletons in and around the waterfront area. Although a dozen or so bodies were found on what was the beach, many more were found in a large boat house in the sea wall. One contained forty skeletons, including that of a horse, and another chamber had twenty-six skeletons. Some of the bodies were huddled up together. What did all this mean? It seems that these people, for whatever reason, were slow in leaving the town. By the time they rushed down to the waterfront and saw the wild, crashing sea, they realized it was too late to escape. In desperation they crowded into the boat house hoping to shelter while the crisis passed. Whether or not they were overcome by fumes before the fiery mud sealed them in, we shall never know.

Experts have worked on the bones of these skeletons and obtained information such as the person's sex, age, and state of health. Scientists are able to piece this information together and come up with possible background information. For example, a young person who showed signs of the medical condition osteoarthritis was used to hard work and might well have been a slave. One of the bodies on the beach had a belt around it with a *gladius*—a legionary sword. Perhaps he was a soldier on leave who was helping people to the shelter when he was struck down.

After World War II

It was a guiding principle of Fiorelli and his successors that, where possible, discoveries such as frescoes and mosaics should be left in the houses where they were found. However, during World War II (1939–45), this principle proved very expensive. In 1943 an Allied air raid dropped 162 bombs on Pompeii by mistake, destroying several homes and their contents. The following year Vesuvius erupted again, scattering over a foot of ash over Pompeii. In recent years Pompeii is again under threat—not from bombs or Vesuvius, but damage from tourists and theft.

Modern Excavations

Excavation has been continued at both Pompeii and Herculaneum. To try to find out more about early Pompeii, the stratigraphical work has continued. In the early 1980s a British archaeologist, Paul Arthur, supervised the digging of a trench. This excavation gave us information about early Pompeii. For example, there were no earlier buildings under the Forum. Also, the amount of simple clay pottery found suggests that until the third century B.C. Pompeii had a small, not particularly well-off, population.

▲ The Forum of Pompeii was an important meeting place for politicians. It was also used as a marketplace.

◄ Herculaneum's Basilica, a Roman town hall. The Basilica contained offices and the magistrates' courts. It was also a meeting place for businesspeople and was usually the most important and expensive public building in town.

Homes versus History

The big issue at Herculaneum is, of course, expansion of the area of excavation. Resina is a crowded, bustling modern town and the townspeople do not want to be pushed out by archaeologists. However, some progress has been made—when apartments and houses have become available they have been bought, which allows a few more feet of rock to be cut back. Recent work has been to the north in the area around the Basilica and the entrance to the Forum. In 1994 rock in the old waterfront area was removed.

Threat from Tourists, Thieves, and Nature

Amedeo Maiuri said that the future of Pompeii and Herculaneum involved a "complex, laborious, slow, and costly work of preservation, protection, and restoration." This has proved very accurate, for Pompeii is facing a serious crisis of preservation.

The threat comes from the thousands of tourists that visit throughout the year. Unfortunately, not all the visitors treat the site with respect. There have been examples of vandalism, particularly the writing of graffiti on frescoes.

Pompeii is a difficult site to protect because it is so large. Despite dog patrols, artifacts are stolen. One archaeologist has gone so far as to call the crisis "the second death of Pompeii." In 1990, armed robbers broke into the storeroom at Herculaneum and stole at least 250 artifacts, including jewelry from the skeletons on the beach.

Another problem for the conservation of the sites is the weather. Even after the work of Fiorelli and others to put up shelters over important areas on the sites, the sun, wind, and rain are still major factors in damage to the exposed areas. Under the layers of ash and rock, the sites had been safe. Now after various bungled excavations in the early years, and work since, the sites are open to the elements. It is a major task to protect the delicate discoveries. Also, the threat of other eruptions and earthquakes are a worry.

▲ It is not surprising that parts of Pompeii are being damaged when tourists clamber over the remains, even the plaster casts of the victims, every year.

A superb snake-design armlet, owned by a rich Pompeiian woman, possibly Sabina Poppea. This expensive gold jewelry was worn on the upper arm. Artifacts like this were the target of thieves in 1990. ▶

Roman Life: Evidence from the Towns

▲ Large numbers of breakable objects, such as these clay wine jugs and pots, have been found in both sites. They have been found in such good condition because the layers of ash or rock sealed Pompeii and Herculaneum away and protected the sites from digging and building damage.

For archaeologists excavating towns and cities of the Roman Empire there are usually a number of problems. The most common is that they were often built over by later settlements right up to the present day. Any attempt to find Roman layers means going down through 15 to 20 feet of ground that contains debris and remains from the past 2,000 years (not to mention modern gas pipes, electricity cables, telephone cables, and sewers). Towns in the countryside that were abandoned at the end of the Roman Empire have usually been covered with soil, and fields have been planted over them. Artifacts, such as pottery and jewelry, are present in the soil, but they have to be sought very carefully.

Why Are These Towns Special?

These difficult archaeological problems at other sites are what make Pompeii and Herculaneum so important as well as unique. The sites have been preserved as they were in A.D. 79. Pompeii has not even been built over. The sites are rich in artifacts, and the houses have been found as they were left nearly 2,000 years ago.

Herculaneum is more of a problem because of the town of Resina above it. The building work and traffic of a modern town might have damaged the site below, but the unique rock layer protects the ancient Roman town.

Preserved Evidence

Chapter two described what Pompeii and Herculaneum were like on the morning of August 24, A.D. 79 before Vesuvius erupted. We know those events happened and certain actions took place—even what food was being served for lunch—because archaeologists have found the evidence. The two towns are unique time capsules that tell us what living in the Roman Empire in the first century A.D. was like.

▲ This painting by Raffaele Gianetti (1832–1916) depicts a street scene in Pompeii before the disaster. The evidence of Roman life found at both Pompeii and Herculaneum give a fascinating insight into the lifestyle, dress, house design, and decoration in the ancient Roman Empire.

What We Have Learned about Roman Life

Although the towns are different in character, we have been able to learn about how the inhabitants earned their livings and spent their time. Pompeii had a number of businesses, providing many goods and services. There were bakeries (complete with mills to grind the corn), wine bars, wine shops, snack bars, fullers' shops, fruit and vegetable stalls, and olive-oil sellers.

The people of Herculaneum had a close relationship with the sea, since the town was on the coast and a number of its population were fishermen. Well-preserved fishing nets have been found with the bronze instruments for mending them.

Roman Leisure Time

A very good picture has emerged of what people did in their spare time. Both towns had theaters—it is believed a rehearsal was taking place on stage at Herculaneum at the moment of the eruption. Although brutally plundered in the eighteenth century, most experts believe the theater was one of the finest examples in the Empire. At the Great Theater in Pompeii inscriptions tell us that covers were erected to protect spectators from the heat of the sun and during intermissions on hot days they were sprinkled with scented water.

▲ The splendid Gladiator barracks next to the Great Theater in Pompeii. Many excellent finds were discovered there, including human remains, armor, and weapons.

Sports were important for large numbers of the population and not just for spectators. Each town had a *Palaestra*, or gymnasium, and swimming pools. The swimming pool at Pompeii was 100 feet long.

At the *Palaestra*, people lifted weights, ran, jogged, and wrestled. For those who preferred spectator sports, Pompeii, as we know, had an impressive amphitheater that put on Games—gladiator fights, animal hunts, and possibly chariot racing. The gladiators had their own barracks near the Great Theater. On the day of the eruption, 63 people died in the barracks, including two men locked up and forgotten in the cells.

Public Baths

Both towns have excellent examples of public baths, which were very important to the Roman way of life. In fact, they have helped archaeologists learn about the whole process of bathing, because not many examples have survived where all the different rooms—some beautifully decorated—are so well preserved.

Cemeteries

We have been able to find out something of the Pompeiians in death. According to Roman law, *Necropoles*, or cemeteries, had to be positioned outside the city walls. The two main ones—outside the Gate of Herculaneum and the Gate of Nuceria—tell us that rich citizens who lived well were buried well, for their mausoleums are designed to impress the living long after the occupants' deaths! Poorer citizens had to make do with urns containing their ashes buried in the ground.

An archaeologist traces graffiti from a wall in Herculaneum in 1994. Clear plastic film is placed over the words and the letters are traced with a black pen. They can then be translated later. ▼

Living Museums

The towns very quickly come to life as we walk around them today, for Pompeii and Herculaneum are living museums. A quick glance at the graffiti-clad walls—"Here Romula met Staphylus" and "Serena has had enough of Isidore"—makes you think that the inhabitants are not so different from people today. The excavations and preservation of the two towns will continue to be important because of the fascinating insight they give to Roman life.

Time Line

A.D. 62–FIFTEENTH CENTURY	EIGHTEENTH CENTURY

A.D. 62 Serious earthquake damages Pompeii.

August 24, A.D. **79** Eruption of Vesuvius. Outpourings totally cover Pompeii and Herculaneum.

203–1400 Vesuvius erupts at least eleven times during this period.

1709 Joseph Nocerino, known as Enzecchetta, discovers the site of the Theater of Herculaneum while digging a well. It is mistaken by Prince of Elbeuf as a temple. ▼

FIFTEENTH–SIXTEENTH CENTURIES

1400–1600 The Renaissance. Great interest in the ancient Greek and Roman worlds.

1593 Count Muzzio Tuttavilla's underground water channel uncovers part of the buried Pompeii. He mistakes the remains for a villa.

◄ **A bronze statue found at the Herculaneum excavations**

1734–59 The Bourbon king, Charles III, reigns in Naples. He shows great interest in archaeology.

1738 Herculaneum officially rediscovered.

1763 Pompeii officially rediscovered.

1765 Herculaneum shut down and all work concentrated on Pompeii.

◄ **One of the excavated streets of Herculaneum**

This time line sets out important events in connection with
Pompeii and Herculaneum.

| NINETEENTH CENTURY | TWENTIETH CENTURY |

1820s Major finds in Pompeii—the
Forum, the Temple of Fortuna Augusta,
and the Forum Baths. ▶

1860 Italian King Victor
Emmanuel II takes the throne.

1860–1875 Fiorelli
directs excavations.

1864 Fiorelli begins
his technique of
making plaster-cast
figures. ◀

1869 Work begins again at Herculaneum,
abandoned in 1875. ▼

1893 House of the Vettii brothers discovered
in Pompeii.

1910–24 Under Spinazzola the
Street of Abundance is uncovered.

1925 Benito Mussolini seizes
power in Italy.

1924–1961 Amedeo Maiuri directs
excavations.

1927 Work begins again at Herculaneum.

1943 During World War II, Allied bombs
damage Pompeii by mistake.

1950s Beginning of large scale tourism to
the sites.

1980 Skeletons discovered near the beach at
Herculaneum.

1990 Theft of precious finds from the
storeroom at Herculaneum.

Glossary

Alabaster A hard, marble-like, white stone.

Amphitheater An oval, open-air area surrounded by seating, used for spectator sports.

Architect A designer of buildings.

Basilica A Roman public building—a town hall.

Bourbon The European royal family (dynasty) that ruled in Spain, Naples, and Sicily during part of the eighteenth and nineteenth centuries.

Bronze A hard material made of a mixture of copper and other metals, such as tin, that can be melted down and cast in shaped molds.

Bust A sculpture of the head, shoulders, and upper chest of a person.

Conservation Keeping something as it is, usually by protecting it from damage.

Earthquake The violent movement of the earth caused when the land plates, which form the earth's surface, move along a fault line.

Earth tremors Movements of the earth that often act as a warning of forthcoming earthquake or volcanic action in an area.

Excavation A hole or hollow made by digging to unearth buried objects in order to find out information about the past.

Façades The fronts of buildings.

Fascist dictatorship A strict, often brutal system of government, with power in the hands of one person—a dictator.

Figurines Small statues.

Forum A large open space in a Roman town or city, usually surrounded by public buildings.

Fresco A wall-painting using watercolors on wet (or sometimes dry) plaster.

Galleries Narrow tunnels or passageways.

Gladiator A person, usually a slave, trained to fight to the death for public entertainment.

Inscription Carved writing, usually on stone.

Isis An Egyptian goddess whose popularity spread throughout the Roman Empire.

Jupiter The most powerful Roman god; also the god of rain, storms, and thunder. Jupiter sometimes appears as a bull.

Lava The hot melted rock that erupts from a volcano.

Marble A hard crystalline rock that can be polished—often used for sculpture.

Middle Ages The period of history between A.D. 500 and 1500.

Mosaic A surface made of colored clay or marble cubes formed into patterns or pictures.

Pantomime A dramatic performance in ancient Rome involving a dancer and chorus.

Papyri (singular papyrus) The paper-like writing materials made from a grass-like plant.

Plaster of Paris A mixture of gypsum (a calcium mineral) and water that sets hard when mixed.

Shrine A place for people to worship a sacred person or object.

Spoil The waste product of an excavation.

Temple A building or place used for the worship of God or of gods and goddesses.

Theater A building designed for the performance of entertainments, such as plays and operas.

Thermopolium A restaurant serving warm drinks, including wine.

Time capsules Containers, buried in the earth for future discovery, that hold objects and documents that are representative of certain periods in time.

Vatican A separate city-state in Rome. It is the headquarters of the Catholic Church.